FOLLOWING

JESUS

IN THREES

I know of no other person with such a passion for spiritual friendship as Tan Soo-Inn. His description of the Christian life as "following Jesus in the company of friends" excites me and resonates deeply with my own vision for church in the 21st century. In this little book, Soo-Inn develops his thoughts about the place of triads in spiritual formation, and presents his conviction with biblical appeal, practical wisdom, and spiritual insight. It is a timely gift to the church. Read it, consider it, and practise it.

Tony Horsfall
Charis Training, UK

This book is a tremendous blessing because it is not only theologically sound, but also realistic and based on practical experience. Spiritual friendship formed and developed by being vulnerable in a safe environment, alongside disciplined study, contemplation, sharing, and listening (and eating) has helped me to honestly and better discern and obey what the Holy Spirit is saying. Even after ten years, the insights and fond memories of the time I spent in a spiritual friendship triad with Soo-Inn and Sivin remain a blessing.

Paul Long
Pastor, Kelston Community Church, Auckland, New Zealand

One of my mentors shared with me about the blessing of the friendship with his soul mate. So I decided to seek such friendship for myself. The Lord gave me one soul mate soon and then two more a few years later. We enjoyed our quartet friendship for some years till one was called to be with the Lord. As we are growing older the blessing of our triad spiritual friendship is growing in many ways, as Soo-Inn writes in this book. Occasionally our triad friendship becomes a hexadic friendship as our wives are invited to join us.

Koichi Ohtawa
Director, CLSK, Japan

Soo-Inn writes with passion, ease, and clarity on a topic for which he is a practitioner and a strong advocate. Anyone looking for a clear, simple, biblical, and workable friendship model to disciple one another towards Christ-likeness should read it, take it to heart, and put it into practice, and they will encounter Jesus in their midst on the road to Emmaus.

Rev Dr Chuah Seong Peng
Senior Pastor, Holy Light Church (English), Johor Bahru, Malaysia

Soo-Inn is a committed believer in "3-2-1" groups. Such groups are similar to the early Methodist Bands. They were first modelled by the Lord Jesus Christ in His relationship with Peter, James, and John, and are safe places for spiritual friendship and accountability. This book is a useful guide on forming and maintaining such groups. I commend it to those who want to travel with others along the journey of life. It takes commitment, openness, and trust to thrive, but may you be blessed as I have been.

Ivan Tan
Pastor, Wesley Methodist Church, Singapore

There is something uniquely life-giving about sitting face-to-face with two friends to share about our lives, and in the process share life together. Every insight in *3-2-1: Following Jesus in Threes* has risen out of biblical truth practised by imperfect vessels desiring to live faithfully in their calling. I trust that the profound simplicity of this book will contribute to more spiritual friendships flourishing, and as a result life-transforming blessings would overflow beyond the triads to the Church and the world.

Rev Sivin Kit
Lutheran Pastor & PhD Candidate in Religion, Ethics, and Society, University of Agder, Norway

Moving to Singapore a few years ago, I was looking for peer friendships for encouragement and advice. I heard Soo-Inn speak about "triads" and I thought, "That's what I need, and that is a guy I want to be with in a triad!" Since that time, my triad with Soo-Inn and another friend has been one of the great joys of my life.

Doug Erdman
National Director, The Navigators, Singapore

We all need kindred friends who will walk life's journeys together with us. In *3-2-1: Following Jesus in Threes*, Soo-Inn gives us very practical handles on making spiritual friendships work. It shows us how to intentionally connect with one another at the heart level. Best of all, it is doable. The "3-2-1" meeting forces us to pause in the midst of our overcrowded schedules and recalibrate our hearts with fellow pilgrims in an authentic relational setting. I recommend this book to anyone seeking spiritual friendship.

Lam Kok Hiang
Country Leader, Cru Singapore

In a world that seems to be more connected than ever, there is a growing disconnectedness and a lack of true relationships. *3-2-1* is a timely reminder and a much-needed wake-up call to return to relationships rightly centred around Christ, that the church might be rooted and built up in Him. In clear, simple, and concise writing, Soo-Inn shares both the whys and hows of spiritual friendship. Enjoy the book and begin your "3-2-1" countdown to meaningful times of following Christ with one another.

Rev Henson Lim
Deputy Senior Pastor, Covenant Vision Christian Church,
Singapore

Friendship in our broken world brings healing, help, and hope to us all. Soo-Inn's method of spiritual friendship in a triad provides a wonderful, simple, and fun way to bring God's Kingdom on earth as it is in heaven, following Jesus' mandate to make disciples of all people.

Judith Davids
Pastoral Counselor, Spiritual Director, and Retreat Leader,
Houston, Texas, USA

Friends in a Broken World
Leadership: A Primer
Making Sense
Spiritual Friendship: A Primer
Thinking on the Run
Travel Mercies

3

FOLLOWING

2

JESUS

1

IN THREES

Soo-Inn Tan

GRACEW♥RKS

Published by Graceworks Private Limited
22 Sin Ming Lane
#04-76 Midview City
Singapore 573969
E-mail: enquiries@graceworks.com.sg
Website: www.graceworks.com.sg

Design by Art4Soul

ISBN: 978-981-07-6615-3

Printed in Singapore

4 5 6 7 8 9 10 • 22 21 20 19 18 17 16 15

CONTENTS

I call it the "ah-ha" discovery of my ministry. A friend of mine says that "we learn by bumping into things". Frankly, I bumped into the value and practice of triads or groups of threes almost 30 years ago and I still consider it my most important "revelation". People grow best in groups of threes (and fours as well).

I have primarily practised triads and quads in the context of intentional discipleship relationships with relational transparency as a key ingredient to processing and applying the foundational truth of God's Word in our lives. Soo-Inn Tan has taken the same practice and applied it to Christian friendship. You might call what my friend Soo-Inn proposes as "mutual mentoring". His application of the threes to intentional friendship creates an environment of deep, trusting, safe relationships, which are critical to our quality of life and an expression of what it means to be created in the image of God.

As I read through this very practical work, a number of descriptive words came to me:

1. **Simple**: We grow together through conversation. One of the first things I noticed in my triad experience was that a group of three was about mutual exchanges, whereas a group of ten would typically require significant leadership training to handle the complexities of group dynamics. We can all engage in meaningful conversation with very simple guidelines (which Soo-Inn provides). I often find myself apologising to those I am teaching by saying, "What I am proposing to you is profoundly simple." The concept behind *3-2-1* is profoundly simple. Yet that is its genius.

2. **Doable**: Soo-Inn's "3-2-1" formula of three people meeting two hours, once a month, is doable in the push and pull of urban life. We can actually carve out the necessary time to make this happen. That is no small feat, given the demands on our life with family, work, and the energy of the city.

3. **Necessary**: Unless we have people in our life with whom we can share our soulful longings and deepest regrets, we do not have the environment in which to be transformed into Christ-likeness. The soil or environment in which our lives take shape is the deep mutual interchange with others on the shared journey of following Jesus.

4. **Purposeful**: So often even the best of friendships can devolve into getting together to just catch up and talk about everyday things. It can start to feel trivial. Soo-Inn describes key components that use the two hours in a balanced way to share our joys and challenges, help each other discern God's will for our life, apply our faith to family, work, and society, and to intercede in prayer for one another.

5. **Complete**: After reading 3-2-1, I thought, "I have everything I need right here to pull off the practice of Christian friendship." Soo-Inn provides both an overview of spiritual friendship, as well as guidelines for maximising these precious two hours every month.

Soo-Inn attributes me as the one who first got him on the concept and value of threes. As one who has been teaching this for years, I am always surprised and pleased as to how my students exceed their teacher. As I read his application to friendship, I found myself saying, "I never thought of just applying the gathering in threes to the mutual mentoring that comes with simple friendship." I got locked inside my discipleship paradigm, while Soo-Inn opened up my world to the practice of growing friendships intentionally, supporting each other as faithful followers of Jesus. This book has now become a part of my toolbox and I can't wait to add this option to my life and impart them to my students.

Greg Ogden
Speaker, Teacher, and Writer on Discipleship

I teach on spiritual friendship a lot. I remind people that we need friends, and that followers of Jesus in particular need to follow Him in the company of like-minded friends, i.e. spiritual friends. This message resonates with many in the increasingly lonely world of the Third Millennium.

Invariably, many who hear me teach on this will affirm that they need spiritual friends but they have no time to develop spiritual friendships. How can we practise the discipline of spiritual friendship in today's busy world? I wanted to come up with a doable model for spiritual friendship.

Are you too busy to meet up with friends? Well, we all need to eat. Jesus spent a lot of time connecting over meals. Why not meet up with friends for a meal? Jesus had twelve disciples but He gave extra time to a group of three: Peter, James, and John. In my readings, I began to see more and more authors suggesting the triad as a basic unit for community.

Three friends meeting over a meal is an achievable way to experience spiritual friendship. "3-2-1" is a simple summary of the concept — *three* friends meeting *two* hours *one* time a month over a meal. "3-2-1" is also an easy catchphrase for people to remember the concept.

This short book contains all you need to understand and practise a 3-2-1 approach to spiritual friendship. It seeks to explain both the whys and hows of 3-2-1 triads. Spiritual friendship is a relationship, not a programme. As such, the material here is not so much prescriptive as it is to provide encouragement, as well as general guidelines.

It is my hope that all of us will journey through life with friends. I trust that this simple book will help.

Friendship is one of the basic needs of life. In his book *Vital Friends*,[1] Tom Rath notes the critical importance of friends for things ranging from good health, healthy marriages and personal growth, to work satisfaction and productivity. Rath concludes:

> ...friendships are among the most fundamental of human needs. The fact is, we are biologically predisposed to this need for relationships, and our environment accentuates this every day. Without friends, it is very difficult for us to get by, let alone thrive.[2]

THE BIBLE AND FRIENDSHIP

The Bible has always been clear about our need for friends. Its teaching on the importance of friendship is very prominent in the Wisdom books.[3] Proverbs 17:17 tells us, "A friend loves at all times, and a brother is born for a time of adversity". While friend and brother stand with us through the ups and downs of life, we cannot choose the family we are born into. But we have to choose our friends and choose to commit ourselves to them. The book of Ecclesiastes, perhaps the most realistic book in the Bible, appeals to us to walk through life with friends.

Two are better than one,
    because they have a good return for their labor:
If either of them falls down,
    one can help the other up.
But pity anyone who falls
    and has no one to help them up.
Also, if two lie down together, they will keep warm.
    But how can one keep warm alone?
Though one may be overpowered,
    two can defend themselves.
A cord of three strands is not quickly broken.
(Ecclesiastes 4:9–12)

Jesus Himself confirms the importance of friendship when He describes His relationship with His disciples as one of friendship (John 15:12–17). Jesus also defines for us the nature of true friendship: "Greater love has no one than this: to lay down one's life for one's friends" (John 15:13). Jesus then commands His disciples to love each other in this way, to be true friends to each other.

FOLLOWING JESUS IN THE COMPANY OF FRIENDS
Indeed, the Christian life can be described as following Jesus in the company of friends. Jesus calls us to follow Him (Luke 9:23–24). He also takes pains to set up a community (Luke 6:12–16) so that His followers follow Him in the context of community. Friends in Christ help each other in their common journey of following Christ.

In Romans 8:29 Paul tells us that God's people were chosen "to become like his Son" (NLT); to be Christ-like. And verses like 1 Thessalonians 5:11 tell us that we are to "build each other up". Friends in Christ help each other in their common journey towards Christ-likeness. Paul J. Wadell describes such "spiritual friendship" as

> a discipleship life, a way in which people who are committed to growing in Christ help one another imitate Christ and grow in gospel virtues.

> Spiritual friends, through their life together, learn from one another what discipleship means and how we can acquire and develop the attitudes and virtues of Christ — they help each other become better friends of God.[4]

In other words, spiritual friendship is friendship that is rooted in Christ for the purpose of helping followers of Jesus grow in Christ. But there is one problem. How do we find the time to build and sustain spiritual friendships in the context of the busy lives that most of us live today? We will look at one simple way that will allow many of us to experience the spiritual friendship we need.

Authentic friendships take time to develop and need time to be nurtured. While the tools of electronic media like e-mail and Facebook may help augment face-to-face contact between friends, they cannot take the place of personal encounters. The apostle John understood the power of letters but he was also clear that certain levels of communication could only happen in person.

> I have much to write to you, but I do not want to use paper and ink. Instead, I hope to visit you and talk with you face to face, so that our joy may be complete. (2 John 1:12)

FRIENDSHIP TAKES TIME

God has made us embodied beings and that means that the best human communication takes place when our bodies show up. But such communication takes time. Richard Lamb summarises this reality well—

time is the currency of relationships... No small-group experience, no friendship, has indelible impact immediately, and lasting relationships are built over years full of hours... Building deep friendships... will probably involve time spent on one another's home turf, an openness to invite people into our lives and the willingness to spend even prime time to deepen the friendship.[5]

This then is the dilemma we face. We need spiritual friendships to follow Jesus healthily. But spiritual friendships, like all good friendships, need time to be nurtured. How then are we to find the time we need for this key relationship? By realising that we can only have a few intimate spiritual friends and investing the time we need with these few friends.

In *The Search to Belong*, Joseph R. Myers proposes that people belong to each other in four kinds of groups: public, social, personal, and intimate.[6] Citing the work of Myers, Jimmy Long explains the nature of the four kinds of groupings.

An example of a **public** space in society would be one of the large sporting events where people come together with one thing in common: rooting for the same team...In the church the large worship gatherings are our public spaces. Even though we may be a diverse congregation, when we worship together, we share a sense of belonging.

The **social** spaces are the places we most neglect in church...These (are) important spaces for informal social interaction, making people feel like they were part of a larger community...In the South, the old Sunday evening potluck suppers were important social spaces in the church.

The small-group community is an ideal **personal** space. Most people who are considering their need to belong to a community will eventually look for some type of small-group community, formal or informal.

The **intimate** spaces are reserved for best friends or spouses. The intimate space is the place where you can share anything and the person will still love you. While it is appropriate to consider what to share in the other three spaces (public, social, personal), in the intimate space we can share our whole self.[7]

SPIRITUAL FRIENDS AS INTIMATE FRIENDS

Interestingly, Jesus also connected to His community by differentiating between these four types of groups.

First, He ministered to the crowds (e.g. Mark 2:13). These were large groups of people who did not know Jesus personally but who were united by their desire to hear His teaching and to receive His ministry. From the crowds He related to a smaller group of seventy-two (or seventy), as mentioned in Luke 10:1. Presumably this group would have more in common among them as compared to the crowds. This was a group that qualified to be sent out for ministry. The third group that Jesus related to was the twelve disciples (Luke 6:12–16). He invested the bulk of His time with this small group. Indeed, the focus of His discipling was the three-year road trip He shared with the twelve. Then there was a fourth group He related to — an intimate group of three: Peter, James, and John (e.g. Mark 9:2). He spent His most significant time with this last group.

Jesus operated within these different circles of relationships. He did not and could not invest the same amount of time in all the people from these four types of groups, and neither can we. Spiritual friends then are to be found in our equivalents of the small groups and especially the intimate groups of our lives. We cannot connect with all our friends with the same degree of intensity. But there will be those "two or three people, in whose lives we are called to be vitally active and extravagantly loving".[8] We need a simple, doable discipline to connect meaningfully with these two or three intimate friends.

CHAPTER 3

THE LOGIC OF FRIENDSHIP TRIADS

We need friends. And we need spiritual friends to help us in our commitment to follow Jesus. The nature of intimate spiritual friendships means that such friendship groups will be small. I propose the following: *three friends meeting two hours once a month*. I suggest that all followers of Jesus be in such friendship triads that commit to meet monthly for two hours.

WHY TRIADS?

I was first introduced to the idea of triads (threes) as a basic unit of discipleship by Greg Ogden in his book *Transforming Discipleship*.[9] His approach to discipleship is based on triads, with one person discipling two others. In *Transforming Discipleship* and in a later book, *Discipleship Essentials*, Ogden shares why he thinks triads work better. Here are some of the reasons he gives.

*Triad discipling shifts the model from hierarchical to relational. The greatest factor inhibiting those who are discipled to disciple others (multiplication) is the dependency fostered by one-on-one relationships. The triad/quad on the other hand, view discipleship as a come alongside relationship of a mutual journey toward maturity in Christ. The hierarchical dimension is minimized.

*The most startling difference between one-on-one and threes and fours is the sense of "groupness". The sense of the Holy Spirit being present in our midst occurred much more often in the group versus the one-on-one.

*There is wisdom in numbers. The group approach multiplies the perspectives on Scripture and application to life issues, whereas one-on-one limits the models and experience. By adding at least a third person there is another perspective brought to the learning process. The group members serve as teachers of one another.[10]

Spiritual friendship is more peer mentoring than discipleship but when Ogden talks about triads as enabling a focus on Christ "as the one toward whom all are directing their lives",[11] he has captured the heart of the spiritual friendship agenda.

In his book *Sacred Companions*,[12] David G. Benner writes with a concern for spiritual direction. Benner understands spiritual direction to be

> a prayer process in which a person seeking help in cultivating a deeper personal relationship with God meets another for prayer and conversation that is focused on increasing awareness of God in the midst of life experiences and facilitating surrender to God's will.[13]

But he notes that there are just too many people who need spiritual direction to be helped by individualised spiritual direction. Benner wants to see the rise of spiritual accompaniment groups and sees such groups as "probably the most readily available means of providing spiritual friendship and direction".[14] Benner's ideal size for such groups? "The optimal size is probably between three and five members."[15]

The triad is not just the basic size for discipleship (Ogden) and spiritual formation (Benner); it is also the basic unit for ministry and mission. In *Culture Making*, Andy Crouch challenges the church to ask:

> What is God doing in culture? What is his vision for the horizons of the possible and the impossible? Who are the poor having good news preached to them?[16]

He then challenges God's people to join God in what He is doing. But Crouch goes on to warn us that we cannot serve God by ourselves. We need to be in community. He writes,

> no matter how complex and extensive the cultural system you may consider, the only way it will be changed is by an absolutely small group of people who innovate and create a new cultural good. The optimal size of this small group? I suggest three. Sometimes it is four or five, and even two can occasionally pull it off. But three is the perfect number.[17]

Crouch challenges all of us to find our "three", "an absolutely small group of people whom you know and trust, with whom you share passion and conviction and commitment, with complementary gifts, talents and needs",[18] as the first step to get involved in what God is doing in the world.

We see then that from discipling to spiritual accompaniment and mission, "three" seems to be the basic building block. Again, modern scholars are discovering what was already Jesus' methodology. We tend to focus so much on Jesus' twelve disciples that we sometimes forget that He paid special attention to an inner circle of three — Peter, James, and John. Even in Jesus' time, a triad was the smallest group for those who wanted to follow Him.

WHY TWO HOURS ONCE A MONTH?
The curse of modern society is busyness. We need an approach to spiritual friendship that is doable. I am not suggesting that 3-2-1 groups replace other groups in a believer's life. I am recommending meeting two other friends for two hours once a month as the bare minimum for the intimate friendships we need. More will be great. But 3-2-1 will be

a must. Even Jesus has promised that "where two or three gather in my name, there am I with them" (Matthew 18:20).

I CHOSE TO BE
IN THIS TRIAD BECAUSE...

CHAPTER 4

THE PRACTICE OF SPIRITUAL FRIENDSHIP

Triads are a simple and doable way of doing spiritual friendship, or "friendship that is rooted in Christ for the purpose of helping followers of Jesus grow in Christ". But what do spiritual friends do? What practices shape a spiritual friendship? Three, at least: loving, supporting, and challenging.

LOVING

Spiritual friends love each other. There are four Greek words for love.[19] Two of them, *agape* and *phileo*, are integral to spiritual friendship. While the two terms overlap to some degree in their usage in New Testament times, *agape* love is the unmerited, sacrificial love one has for another. Such love may not be reciprocated. *Phileo*, however, is more often translated as the love between friends, a mutual affection where care is both given and received. In John 15:13, Jesus integrates these two types of love: "Greater love has no one than this: to lay down one's life for one's friends". As Jesus defines it, friendship is to be defined by mutual unmerited sacrificial love.

Love can be expressed in many ways but two expressions in particular are crucial for spiritual friendship. First, in love, friends accept each other. Friends must obey the biblical injunction to "Accept one another, then, just as Christ accepted you" (Romans 15:7). As friends get to know each other better, they will discover each other's strengths and weaknesses. Because their love for each other is unmerited, friends do not judge and condemn each other. They may hate the sin, but they always love and accept their friend. Hence spiritual friendships are safe places — places where I can be myself.

The second key expression of friendship love is forgiveness. Spiritual friends forgive when they have been wronged by their friends. In any ongoing relationship where there is true intimacy, there will be times when friends hurt each other because of ignorance, immaturity, or sin. For the relationship to survive, and to grow, spiritual friends must be committed to obeying Paul's command in Ephesians

4:32: "Be kind and compassionate to one another, forgiving each other, just as in Christ God forgave you". As Paul Wadell reminds us:

> How could we live together at all if we are not able to forgive and be forgiven? All the pivotal relationships of our lives could have broken down forever if we were not able to reach out to one another in forgiveness.[20]

SUPPORTING

Because friends love each other, they are there for each other in the hard times of life. Friends carry each other's burdens (Galatians 6:2). We all experience the brokenness of a fallen world in different ways. We count on our friends to stand with us and help us in the crushing moments of life. Indeed it is often in the difficult moments of life that we discover who our true friends are. Spiritual friendship is a statement against the competitive individualism that still characterises much of modern society. It is not good for man to be alone (Genesis 2:18). Hence the biblical reminder that two are better than one and indeed, three is even better (Ecclesiastes 4:9–12).

Apart from practical acts of assistance, there are two key ways that friends can support each other in the difficult moments of life: empathise with one another and encourage one another. Romans 12:15 tells followers of Jesus to "Rejoice with those who rejoice; mourn with those who mourn". Emotions are a key part of our humanity. Having friends who will rejoice with us in our times of celebration and who will weep with us in our sorrow will help us to be emotionally healthy. That is what Job's friends did for him when they heard about his tragedies (Job 2:11–13). Ironically it was when they opened their mouths and tried to suggest solutions that they became unhelpful.

And above all, friends are encouragers. Paul reminds us in 1 Thessalonians 5:11 that we are to "encourage one another and build each other up". When friends are in trouble, we help, we empathise, and we encourage them by pointing them to the Lord. We note that Paul encourages the Thessalonians with good theology.[21] The encouragement that spiritual friends offer to one another is not based on human assurances but is rooted in God and His Word.

CHALLENGING

Finally, spiritual friends challenge each other to grow in the Lord. We see this linkage between caring and challenging for growth in 1 Thessalonians 5:11 where encouragement is linked to "building each other up". If I truly love my friend, I must accept him unconditionally. But I also want him to grow in Christ-likeness and to fulfil his potential in Christ. Spiritual friends are particularly well placed to encourage growth in each other because their relationship is built on a foundation of love and a history of having borne one another's burdens. How do friends help each other grow in the Lord?

First, they teach each other (Romans 15:14). This may include working through a book together. But often the most effective kind of learning is reflecting on life's experiences in the light of the Word, and guided by the Spirit. The triad provides a context where friends learn about God and about life through sharing with each other the stories of what they have learnt from the crucible of their own lives.

Friends also admonish one another if they see a friend moving in a direction that is sinful or holds the potential for sin. They gently rebuke a friend when that person is wandering away from the path of Christ. Friends live out what James writes at the end of his letter:

> My brothers and sisters, if one of you should wander from the truth and someone should bring that person back, remember this: Whoever turns a sinner from the error of their way will save them from death and cover over a multitude of sins. (James 5:19–20)

Besides that, friends cheer each other on in their common quest to follow Christ. They "spur one another on toward love and good deeds" (Hebrews 10:24). Most of the time we know what we should do. But we lack the encouragement and the accountability to put into practice what we know. Spiritual friends help me to do what I should do and to be what I should be.

> One of the great gifts of a good friendship is that each friend helps the other grow in

freedom by helping them be more fully and authentically who they are called to be.[22]

These then are the three primary practices of spiritual friendship — loving, supporting, and challenging. We will now look at three basic spiritual disciplines that help give expression to spiritual friendship.

Triads provide a context for friends in Christ to help each other grow in Christ-likeness. They do it through loving, supporting, and challenging. And to make this happen, the members of a triad need to be committed to three basic spiritual disciplines: listening, sharing, and discernment.

LISTENING

In his classic book on Christian community, Dietrich Bonhoeffer reminds us that the primary ministry that we offer one another in community is the ministry of listening.

> The first service that one owes to others in fellowship consists in listening to them. Just as love to God begins with listening to His Word, so the beginning of love for the brethren is learning to listen to them.[23]

James 1:19 tells us that we are to be quick to listen, slow to speak and slow to anger. As Bonhoeffer reminds us, listening is an expression of love: "To listen is to validate, acknowledge, and appreciate another person".[24] Unfortunately there is little in our education that teaches us how to listen. Thomas R. Hawkins has this to say about listening.

> Listening requires suspending our own agendas, forgetting about what we want to say...Listening is attentive receptivity toward another person. To listen we suspend our own agendas and immerse ourselves in the other person.[25]

We listen because we value the people we are listening to. It is hard work. We live in an increasingly hectic and lonely world. Most of us rush through our days without anyone really listening to us. The triad should function as a relational oasis where friends bless each other with the gift of listening.

SHARING OUR STORIES

Listening and sharing are two parts of one reality. If we are to listen, someone has to share. And it is in listening and sharing that friendship is forged.

Community is formed only by shared stories, not by monologues. Empathetic listening is followed, in time, by reciprocal storytelling. I know I have a place in the community not only as I hear and accept its stories but as it hears and makes room for mine.[26]

The triad works only if there is a high degree of honest sharing between its members. Roberta Hestenes points out in *Using the Bible in Groups* that human communication can be divided into five levels.

Level 1: Cliché conversation. This is the superficial chitchat level of talking which focuses on safe topics such as the weather, sporting events, local happenings, etc.

Level 2: Sharing of information and facts. At this level people talk about events, ideas and facts, but not yet really about themselves.

Level 3: Sharing of ideas and opinions. There is more willingness at this level to share one's own personal ideas and opinions. This takes a bit more risk.

Level 4: Sharing of feelings. At this level people are willing to risk telling other (people)... what they are feeling, not just what they are thinking. These feelings may be positive or negative.

Level 5: Peak communication. This is the deepest level of communication when (people)... experience strongly their sense of belonging and sharing...without defensiveness or barriers. Openness, transparency, and self-disclosure shapes the flow of the conversation (at this level).[27]

Normal human communication includes all five levels of communication. But triads are places where one can communicate at the deepest levels if need be. We see Jesus modelling this level of honest sharing when He shares with His closest friends what He is feeling during His travail in the Garden of Gethsemane, and His need for them:

Then Jesus went with them to a place called Gethsemane, and he said to the disciples, "Sit here while I go over there and pray." He took with him Peter and the two sons of Zebedee, and became anguished and distressed. Then he said to them, "My soul is deeply grieved, even to the point of death. Remain here and stay awake with me." (Matthew 26:36–38, NET)

DISCERNING

Triad members open their lives to each other but they must do so with the understanding that their lives are lived under the authority of the Word of God. That means that sharing and listening, the foundational practices of triads, must always be accompanied by discernment. By listening with biblical discernment, triad members ensure that the triad is not just for helping people feel good. They exist to encourage growth in Christ-like maturity. In *Soul Talk*, Larry Crabb reminds us that genuine dialogue between Christian friends must aid the sanctification process. We need to walk with people through the ups and downs of their lives. But we still need to hold people responsible to live by God's truth. In response to what he sees as the modern concern for empathy over the older concern for biblical admonishment he writes:

Should we then not talk to people about their responsibility to obey biblical principles in their specific situation? Is feeling people's pain and wanting to heal wounds that cause the pain a bad thing? Can't we do both, first empathize then guide or exhort?[28]

In 1 Thessalonians 5:19–22 (NET), Paul writes:

Do not extinguish the Spirit. Do not treat prophecies with contempt. But examine all things; hold fast to what is good. Stay away from every form of evil.

Paul may have been writing to guide a church community but his exhortation is also applicable to triads. There must be an openness where we do not quench the sharing that takes place in the triad. Sharing is essential for the life of the triad. When someone shares, we need to listen carefully and discern. We need to have our stories sifted by the Word of God.

THE SPIRITUAL DISCIPLINES THAT I HAVE
MORE CHALLENGES WITH ARE...

MY THOUGHTS ON HOW TO GROW
IN THESE AREAS...

CHAPTER 6

BASIC COMPONENTS OF A 3-2-1 MEETING

The idea for a triad meeting is simple enough. Three followers of Jesus bond in an intimate friend-ship to help them better follow Christ. They meet once a month for about two hours. They listen, share, and discern. But what actually happens in a triad meeting? Since a triad is relationship and not a programme, what happens in a triad meeting cannot be scripted in detail. However, triad meetings should contain some basic components. Three are fundamental: meals, spiritual conversations, and prayer.

MEALS
I strongly suggest that a triad meeting take place over a meal; a proper meal like lunch or dinner. The importance of meals for Christian life is clearly seen in the Bible. Commenting on Paul's teaching on meals and community, Robert Banks notes:

The meal that they shared together reminded the members of their relationship with Christ and one another and deepened those relationships...[29]

There are practical reasons to meet over a meal. Folks who live in urban contexts often struggle to find a common time to meet up. Having meals is already in our calendars. It is just a matter of making a decision to eat together.

Meals also express friendship in a concrete way. Christine D. Pohl reminds us:

Because eating is something every person must do, meal-time has a profoundly egalitarian dimension... Meal-time, when people sit down together, is the clearest time of being with others, rather than doing for others.[30]

Having a meal together is the best context for a triad meeting. As we eat we slow down, we welcome each other, we leave our hectic schedules behind us for a while, and we share our lives.

CONVERSATIONS

The heart of the meeting will be the practice of meaningful conversation, where we speak truth lovingly and give each other the gift of empathetic listening.

> ...it may be that conversation is the greatest gift of community and the fundamental means by which community in the Spirit is attained...it is (through) the conversation of friends...that we grow in wisdom, grace and strength.[31]

Trust takes time to build. Initially the members of the triad could share one joy and one struggle they had experienced since they last met. Sharing one joy and one struggle gives a snapshot of one's soul and, done on a regular basis, helps the group's members get to know each other.

As the triad members grow in their trust for each other, they can give updates on what is happening in the key areas of their lives, for example, their personal walk with God, church life, key relationships (e.g. with spouse, children), and work life. Such sharing provides the opportunity for members to practise spiritual friendship, love, support, and challenge each other (see Chapter 4). As they share and listen, they can support each other (bear burdens, empathise, encourage) and challenge each other to grow (teach, admonish, spur one another towards love and good deeds). The stuff of daily life is the raw material with which we fashion our life in Christ, and the triad functions as a relational crucible for this to happen.

PRAYER

The third basic component for triad meetings is prayer. This is the one activity that expresses the reality that the triad friendship is one that is based on a common friendship with Jesus. Of course the whole meeting should be one where the three are conscious of the presence of the Christ who promised: "where two or three gather in my name, there am I with them" (Matthew 18:20). But sometime during the meeting, the triad focuses on God and communes with Him. Our communion with each other and with Him are inextricably intertwined.

When we enter the...dimension of prayer together we gain deep insights into each others' needs and strengths. Conversely, when we know each other, and are committed to friendship, our prayers become profound and real.[32]

Indeed prayer is a natural response to the issues arising from the conversations. It is an acknowledgement that our lives are lived in total dependence on the Lord. Traditionally, Christian prayer has been divided into four components, summarised by the acronym "ACTS".

* **A**doration — Affirming of the character of God, His love, His holiness, His majesty.

* **C**onfession — Acknowledging our moral shortcomings before the Lord and seeking appropriate forgiveness.

* **T**hanksgiving — Remembering and thanking God for the specific ways He blesses us.

* **S**upplication — Bringing our cares and the cares of others before the Lord.[33]

One or more of the four components may need special focus, depending on what has been discussed during the meeting. And sometimes there may be the need for periods of silence to hear what the Lord may be saying in our conversation with Him.

If the triad is meeting in a public place, they will need to find creative ways to pray without attracting unnecessary attention. They could pray with their eyes open, speaking in a normal conversational tone. Any onlookers will think the three are in a conversation, which they are — with the Lord.

These then are the three basic components of triad meetings: eating together, sharing life through conversation, and praying together. The meeting should end with the three fixing the date and time of the next triad meeting. Such meetings may look simple but when three friends who commit themselves to each other and to the Lord meet in this way, month by month, over time, powerful transformation takes place.

MY PRAYER FOR THIS
FRIENDSHIP TRIAD IS...

The fundamental activities of a triad meeting are sharing meals, conversations, and prayer. At first glance, triad meetings seem extraordinarily simple. But God uses the ordinary to accomplish His extraordinary goals. As a triad meets, once a month, month by month, lives are transformed and relationships are strengthened. And as the triad members grow in their trust of each other, the triad can also become a safe place for three key spiritual disciplines: confession, decision-making, and vocational discernment.

CONFESSION

James 5:16 tells us:

> Therefore confess your sins to each other and pray for each other so that you may be healed.

Those in the Roman Catholic tradition follow the practice of confessing their sins to a priest. But fcw in most traditions obey James' injunction for followers of Jesus to confess their sins to one another. Clearly we need to be wise in choosing who we go to for such an exercise. A triad group holds the promise of the safety of deep friendships that make such confessions possible. Dietrich Bonhoeffer would also argue that it is when we confess our sins to each other that true fellowship actually happens. True fellowship requires transparency. When we acknowledge our sins to one another we are truly transparent.

> In confession the break-through to community takes place. Sin demands to have a man by himself. It withdraws him from the community. The more isolated a person is, the more destructive will be the power of sin over him, and the more deeply he becomes involved in it, the more disastrous is his isolation...In confession the light of the Gospel breaks into the darkness and seclusion of the heart...Since the confession of sin is made in the presence of a Christian brother, the last stronghold of self-justification is abandoned.[34]

Mutual confession is one key spiritual discipline that has been neglected by the church. We can only wonder how many followers of Jesus would have avoided falling into sin if this were practised more regularly in our communities. I think of our leaders in particular, many of whom are tired and lonely, and vulnerable.

Friends who have the privilege of hearing a friend's confession have the privilege of assuring the confessing friend he or she has been forgiven, on the basis of Bible promises like 1 John 1:8–9. The on-going friendship is also a context for help in dealing with temptation, and the healing of the wounds associated with sin, which is the goal of James 5:16.

DECISION-MAKING

The modern world is one that presents many choices. In biblical times, people had less need to make choices. Marriage? Many marriages were arranged ones. Job? You often ended up entering the family business. Today, however, we have the freedom and the responsibility to decide on many issues in our lives, decisions about career, relationships, ministry, etc. The follower of Christ faces such decisions with the desire to do God's will. This is simple where the choices are ones that the Bible addresses directly, e.g. don't murder, don't give false testimony, etc. But many choices are ones that involve more application of biblical principles and often the choices are not that clear.

A community of people who love God, and who love each other, will be a key context to help one make wise biblical decisions. Dr Bruce Waltke puts it well:

> Christian brothers and sisters can help keep us accountable to live as Christians in an un-Christian world. They can ask the hard questions, offer a new perspective, and be used by God to influence our lives. We can seek their counsel when we are unclear from Scripture what God would have us do...[35]

Waltke brings out two points about decision-making that are relevant to triads. First, he points out the key role that Christian friends can play in helping us make decisions. This is biblical:

...let the wise listen and add to their learning,
   and let the discerning get guidance...
   (Proverbs 1:5)

But Waltke also reminds us that community helps keep us accountable to live out what we have decided. Knowing what to do is only half the battle. We need faith and courage to do what we know we should do. "The heart is deceitful above all things" (Jeremiah 17:9a). A triad can help us decide and encourage us to carry out our decisions.

VOCATIONAL DISCERNMENT

Gordon T. Smith reminds us in *Courage & Calling* that every follower of Christ has to answer three calls. They are:

The general call — the invitation to follow Jesus, to be Christian;

The specific call — a vocation that is unique to a person; that individual's mission in the world;

The immediate responsibilities — those tasks or duties God calls us to today.[36]

Triads can help their members discern their vocations. As Smith reminds us, vocational discernment takes place in the context of community.

> But it is also important to stress that our self-knowledge and self-awareness happen in community...In community we come to appreciate our gifts and abilities — by noting and having others note how we contribute to the well-being of the community. In community we see how we are unique and how the desires of our hearts are different than but also affirmed by others.[37]

One of the greatest gifts that triad members can give each other is help to clarify each other's vocation. Waltke defines a call as

> an inner desire given by the Holy Spirit, through the Word of God and confirmed by the community of Christ.[38]

Discovering our calling is key in being good stewards of our lives. Triads can play a key role in helping us to confirm our callings and in providing encouragement and help in carrying out our callings.

Triads provide the relational context for our discipleship. In a triad, friends help each other grow in Christ. They do this by providing a community for three key practices: mutual confession, decision-making, and vocational clarification.

I SENSE A CALLING TO...

SOME AREAS I AM PRAYING FOR
DISCERNMENT ARE...

What actually happens when the three members of a triad come together for a regular meeting? Because 3-2-1 is more of a relationship than a programme, there is no fixed template for 3-2-1 meetings. However, if a meeting is to accomplish its goals, some basic components need to be there. This is what a typical triad meeting could look like.

EATING TOGETHER
The meeting takes place over a meal. Eating together is not a backdrop for the conversations that will take place. It is a critical part of the process. The meal should preferably be in an eating establishment that provides enough quiet and privacy for the meeting. Every meal is sacramental to a degree and the act of saying grace at the beginning of the meal reminds all that indeed Christ is "the unseen guest at every meal, the silent listener to every conversation".

CONNECTING

One easy way for group members to bring each other up to date with each other's lives is for each member to share a major life event that has taken place since the group last met. Alternatively, they can share their responses to a simple examen. Each member of the group shares two things — one item of joy or thanksgiving and an item of concern or prayer — in that person's life at that point in time. This helps the members centre on the state of their hearts, and in sharing, they reconnect with each other spiritually. It also sets the tone for the rest of the meeting.

CHECKING IN

A key part of the meeting is when the members take turns to give updates on what is happening in key areas of their lives. People share what they feel they're comfortable to share, though it is hoped that as the group continues to meet, the trust level will rise and people will grow in their transparency about what they share. Some basic areas for sharing are:[39]

* **Life with God.** This would include updates on how the members are doing in their spiritual disciplines.

* **Life at work.** Work is not just confined to paid employment. For those retired, this could involve volunteer work. Homemakers are similarly engaged in critical work.

* **Family life.** This would include how one is doing in one's key family relationships, e.g. with spouse, children, parents.

* **Life in church.**

One way of sharing about these key areas is, again, to share one joy and one struggle in that particular area. The purpose of giving updates in these areas of life is for the group to help one another process their lives from the perspective of Scripture and to receive encouragement and suggestions as to how one can be more Christ-like in all aspects of life.

GETTING HELP

The group can move on to see if there are any specific areas where one or more of the members may need help. The group will be a place where the members can find encouragement and discernment when they face difficulties in their lives. For example, the group can be a safe place for members to process key decisions they are facing, with people who know them, who are committed to the Lord, and who are committed to helping them grow in the Lord. And as the trust level of the group grows, members can also get help for temptations they are facing. In the event that a member falls into sin, the triad will be a key group to find support and accountability in any journey of repentance and restoration. Prevention is better than cure. Members may have to gently confront each other if they see one of their members doing things that might compromise their walk with the Lord.

The triad is thus a safe place to process the struggles of life so that the group members can grow in the Lord. We are told to:

> Consider it pure joy, my brothers and sisters, whenever you face trials of many kinds, because you know that the testing of your faith produces perseverance. Let perseverance finish its work so that you may be mature and complete, not lacking anything. (James 1:2–4)

This is a command given to a community and it is meant to be carried out in communities like a triad.

STUDYING TOGETHER

If the triad has committed itself to do a study together, they can now move on to discuss what they have studied. A close relational group is an ideal place for learning together. Triads can go through a book together or they can study the Bible together. Studying in a triad provides a context for understanding and for applying what is learnt. Friends keep each other accountable to live out what they believe to be true.

PRAYING TOGETHER

The last major component of the triad meet is praying together. Members can intercede for each other based on the issues that came up during the meeting and/or other items raised at this time. Followers of Christ should be concerned for needs outside of themselves. Time could also be spent interceding for people and situations that the Lord brings to the attention of the group.

SETTING A DATE FOR THE NEXT MEETING

The last thing the group does before the meeting ends is to decide on a date for the next meeting. Since the triad is a major commitment, members understand that regular monthly meetings are a priority. The selected date is a date all group members have agreed upon. It is understood that, barring emergencies, members of the triad will keep the date.

This is how a triad meeting looks like. It is by no means an exhaustive list of possible things that a triad could do. For example, a triad could embark on a ministry project and time would have to be spent discussing how to carry out the project. In addition, triad members can and should connect with each other in between meetings. But if three friends were to just meet up two hours once a month over a meal, and do the things suggested above, I believe they will see God transform their lives in significant ways.

THE BEST PART OF THE 3-2-1 GROUP IS...

How does one go about starting a triad? What is the life cycle of a 3-2-1 group?

CONVICTION

First you must be convicted of the purpose of 3-2-1 groups. This means you must be committed to the goal of growing in Christ-likeness and you must be convicted of the critical importance of intimate spiritual friendship groups in helping one mature in Christ-likeness. 3-2-1 is not another programme. It is a serious commitment to be the person God wants you to be.

ACCOUNTABILITY

Next, you may need to let the relevant authorities in your church know about your plans if your 3-2-1 group is not an official ministry of your church. This is to ensure that your church leaders know what you are trying to do. It would be great if your church could support this initiative with prayer.

PRAYER

You need to commit the whole endeavour to the Lord in prayer. You should also ask the Lord to bring people to mind who could be candidates for membership in your triad.

INVITATION

Invite potential triad members to a meal and share with them the concept of the 3-2-1 group. You could lend each potential member of the triad a copy of this book. Invite them to join you in starting a triad. Ask them to take time to read this book and to pray and ask the Lord if this is something they want to do. The 3-2-1 group requires commitment and so people should join only if they are convicted to do so. After an agreed-upon period, contact these possible triad members to confirm their membership in the triad. If one or both of the initial invitees say no, pray and ask the Lord for fresh names and go through the invitation exercise again.

RUN THE FIRST MEETING

Members new to intimate spiritual friendships may be anxious about what happens at 3-2-1 meetings. Ask them to commit to two meetings for a start. Have a review at the end of the second meeting. Ask fellow group members what they think of the meetings — what went well and what could be improved. You may have to explain to them the purpose and the nuts and bolts of the 3-2-1 groups again.

It is possible that after one or two meetings, one or both members feel that the 3-2-1 group is not for them. Bless them as they leave and encourage them to find community in other groups.

CALL FOR COMMITMENT

At this time potential members are asked if they are willing to commit themselves to the triad. A simple covenant may help to summarise the basic commitments needed to help make the triad work. This is what a covenant may look like:

Sample of u triad covenant

1. **Commitment**

   This spiritual friendship triad is a priority in my life. I will be present at all meetings that have been agreed upon. In the event that I cannot come to a meeting because of an emergency I will inform my triad members as soon as possible.

2. **Edification**

   With the help of the Lord and my friends, I commit myself to helping my group members grow in Christ-likeness.

3. **Acceptance**

   I will practise Jesus' command to accept one another as Christ has accepted us. With the help of the Lord I will accept my group members for who they are. This does not mean that I will agree with everything other group members say but I will respect their opinions and try my best to understand where my triad friends are coming from.

4. **Biblical Authority**

   I understand that the group members will have different opinions on the issues we talk about but on all major matters of faith and practice we understand that the Bible, properly interpreted, will be our final authority.

5. **Confidentiality**

   I understand that friendships are based on honest sharing. Therefore I will play my part in helping my friends to share by keeping in confidence all that I hear in the group meeting. If I want to share with anyone outside the group, I will first get permission from the group.

6. **Transparency**

   I will share my life with my triad members. That means where appropriate, and to the degree I am ready, I will share personal details of my life, my thoughts, feelings, and opinions to help us, the triad, process our lives as a basis for encouragement and growth.

Signed _____ Dated _____

It is critical that the covenant is not one imposed on the triad members. All triad members must help to draft the covenant. Once the covenant has been drafted, all members should commit themselves to it. After two meetings the potential triad members must decide if they are committing themselves to the life of the group.

PERIODIC REVIEWS

Continue to meet at least once a month and have another review in six months. People are more willing to commit to a group when they realise that they are not locked into a commitment of indeterminate duration. After six months, ask the group how they feel — what is working and what can be improved. By then, they should have experienced some of the blessings of the 3-2-1 group and should be motivated to continue.

After the first six-month review, review again in another six months, after the group has been meeting for a year. As before, ask for feedback on the life of the group and ask if the members are willing to commit for another year.

The group may feel led to introduce elements in the life of the group from time to time, like a book study or a ministry project. Such initiatives may come from any member of the group but must be agreed upon by all.

ENDING WELL

Some 3-2-1 groups meet over many years and deep friendships are forged that give vital encouragement to the members in their journey of following Christ. But there are times when a group may have to close. Sometimes the reasons are simple. One or more of the members may move away and may no longer be living in the same town. While communication technology allows people to keep in touch though they are separated geographically, the heart of the 3-2-1 group is the face-to-face meet up. Sometimes one or more of the members may find that they are no longer able to commit themselves to the group because of changes in their life circumstances that result in new demands on their time. Sometimes one or more members feel the need to experience spiritual friendship in another format or with a different group.

Whatever the reason, some or all the members may no longer feel the conviction to carry on. If you are committed to 3-2-1 groups you may have to start the process again and ask the Lord for His guidance to help start a new 3-2-1 group.

A group that has come to the end of its life must end well. There should be a last meeting where members are encouraged to recount highlights in the life of the group and to share how the group has blessed them. There should be opportunities to thank God for His blessings on the group and to thank each other for their contributions to the group. All this will help bring about a proper closure to the group and this will help when starting again with any future groups.

CONCLUSION

In his book *On the Way*, Gordon T. Smith makes a number of points that help explain our commitment to spiritual friendship in small groups. On the value of small groups he writes:

Many Christians find it valuable to be part of a small group that serves as a close community of peers. These groups can take a variety of forms, but ideally a group should meet regularly every week or two for reflection on the Scriptures, sharing of personal concerns (including areas of failure), encouragement and counsel between the participants, and prayer.[40]

On friendship, Smith writes:

> Friendship is the foundational relationship of life. All other relationships are passing and temporal; friendships have the possibility of being eternal...C.S. Lewis stated it well: "Friendship seemed the happiest and most fully human of all loves, the crown of life and the school of virtue".[41]

3-2-1 groups, therefore, are small groups of spiritual friends, journeying alongside each other as they seek to follow Christ.

SOME THOUGHTS

1. **MUST ALL MEMBERS OF A TRIAD BE OF THE SAME GENDER OR ARE MIXED GROUPS OKAY?**

I try not to be dogmatic on issues where there is no direct command from the Bible. God created humankind male and female and good things happen when men and women work in teams. I remember being part of a triad in high school consisting of two guys and a gal. However, the intensity of intimate groups like triads means that they work better if their members are of the same gender. Usually, unless the group members are very mature, there are some things that people are reluctant to share with members of the opposite sex. The depth of sharing expected in triads could also lead to inappropriate emotional bonding between members of the opposite sex. Here is David G. Benner's take on the issue:

> In my experience there is no need to restrict membership to a single gender [but]...

intimacy often develops more quickly when the group is composed only of men or women...[42]

2. CAN TRIADS BE COMPOSED OF THREE COUPLES INSTEAD OF THREE INDIVIDUALS?

I am all for couple support groups. But such couple groups should not take the place of triads. If someone is struggling with a difficult marriage for example, he or she may not be ready to discuss his or her marriage problems in front of his or her spouse, and in front of others. Groups that mix couples and singles may not work too for the same reasons. But a triad provides a safe context for any initial grappling with the issues.

It needs to be said that triads should not be the only group in a believer's life. All of us need to be part of different types of groups that play different roles in our lives.

3. IS THERE ANY IDEAL AGE COMPOSITION FOR THE TRIAD MEMBERS?

Since triads function more like peer accountability groups, the age difference between the members is not as important as the maturity of the group members. What is more important is the compatibility of the people in the group. Besides, age may not necessarily have a direct bearing on the spiritual maturity of a person.

Usually people tend to view those ten years or older than them as from an older generation and no longer a peer. However I have led a number of triads where I was ten years older than the other two members. In many ways I functioned as a leader because I had had more life experience. Because I have lived longer, I have had time to make more mistakes. I made the lessons I had learnt from my life available to them. But the other two had had their own unique life experiences too and brought their own wisdom to the relationship. I learnt so much from them as well.

There is therefore no ideal age difference for the members of a triad. What is more important is the group members' commitment to the purposes of the group and to each other. Such a commitment should be evidenced by a high degree of mutual respect, regardless of the respective ages of the members.

4. DOES A 3-2-1 GROUP REPLACE OTHER FAITH-BASED COMMUNITY GROUPS?

No. While a triad provides a high degree of transparency and accountability it does not provide the diversity that we need in our relationships. In Chapter 2 we saw that people connect in at least four different kinds of groups — large groups, social groups, small groups, and intimate groups. The danger of having a triad as the only group in our lives is that we tend to see the Kingdom of God only through the eyes of our group, but the Kingdom of God is much larger than that.

We need to gather with the whole congregation from time to time to celebrate the diversity of God's people. Social groups are great to connect with a diversity of people and as a first step to building deeper relationships.

God's ideal for His church is diversity. We are to learn from people who are different from us. Old and young, men and women, people of different races and social status...We are to celebrate diversity in our unity in Christ and we are to learn from each other. We will need groups other than our triads for that to happen.

5. CAN IT BE 4-3-2?

Can the group consist of four people meeting for three hours twice a month? Of course. 3-2-1 is not directly prescribed by Scripture and we cannot be dogmatic about it.

However, I don't recommend groups larger than four. Anything beyond four in a group is less ideal for what we are trying to accomplish in our 3-2-1s. The intimacy level tends to drop. It takes longer for the group to gel. And the larger the group the harder to find a common time for the group to meet. Two hours a month is only a suggestion for the bare minimum amount of time needed for any meaningful interaction to take place. Longer meetings are fine if people can give the time.

And more meetings a month are fine, too. But I would encourage groups to meet at least once in six weeks. Otherwise the group tends to lose momentum.

6. AREN'T THREES INWARD LOOKING?

The 3-2-1 groups are aimed specifically at helping members grow in Christ-likeness. And Christ comes to us as a humble servant committed to blessing people (Mark 10:45). If a group is fulfilling its purpose, her members will be energised and encouraged to make a difference in the world through word and deed (Matthew 5:13–16).

7. **HOW MANY THREES CAN I HAVE AT ANY ONE TIME?**

3-2-1 groups require commitment of time, energy, and attention. Realistically it will be hard to commit to more than two groups at any one time.

8. **WHAT HAPPENS IF ALL THE MEMBERS OF A 3-2-1 GROUP ARE VERY YOUNG IN THE FAITH? WE ARE AFRAID THAT WE MIGHT END UP POOLING OUR SPIRITUAL IGNORANCE.**

Triads are not meant to replace other groups. If the members of a triad are young in the faith they may need to be discipled in the context of mentoring relationships in addition to the triad. Or the triad itself could be used as a discipleship group. Greg Ogden has practised and championed an approach to discipling where a more mature Christian disciples two or three others.[43]

In her book *The Top Five Regrets of the Dying*, Bronnie Ware puts "I wish I had stayed in touch with my friends" as the fourth top regret.[44] She records the following words from one of the patients she cared for in her work in palliative care.

> I am missing my friends most of all. Some have died. Some are in situations like me (living in nursing homes). Some I have lost touch with. I wish I hadn't lost touch with them. You imagine your friends will always be there. But life moves on, and suddenly you find yourself with no one in the world who understands you or who knows anything about your history.[45]

We were created for companionship. It is possible to die of loneliness. Our human need for friends would be reason enough to take the pursuit of friendships seriously. Followers of Jesus have even more reason to do so. Brother John of Taize reminds us:

> Although friendship is a universal human reality, there is a particular type of friendship that defines what it means to be a Christian: we are friends of one another because we are friends of Christ...[46]

Like many, Brother John notes the loneliness and individualism of modern society, where relationships are primarily transactional. This is true even in our church communities. This loneliness and individualism "create in many people a longing for simple bonds of acceptance with no ulterior motives, one that is often not met by...families of origin".[47]

3-2-1 groups provide a simple, doable way to walk with friends. While we need the nurturing provided by such triads, more importantly, the triads also encourage us to offer the friendship of Christ to a lonely world — a world lonely for friends, and lonely for God.

ENDNOTES

CHAPTER 1

1. Tom Rath, *Vital Friends* (New York, NY: Gallup Press, 2006).
2. Ibid., 15.
3. In the Old Testament, the books of Proverbs, Job, and Ecclesiastes are collectively known as the Wisdom books, books that were written from God-guided reflection on life experience.
4. Paul J. Wadell, *Becoming Friends* (Grand Rapids, MI: Brazos Press, 2002), 108.

CHAPTER 2

5. Richard Lamb, *Following Jesus in the "Real World"* (Downers Grove, IL: InterVarsity Press, 1995), 95.
6. Joseph R. Myers, *The Search to Belong* (Grand Rapids, MI: Zondervan, 2003).
7. Jimmy Long, *Emerging Hope* (Downers Grove, IL: InterVarsity Press, 2004), 139–140.
8. Lamb, *Following Jesus in the "Real World"*, 84.

CHAPTER 3

9. Greg Ogden, *Transforming Discipleship* (Downers Grove, IL: InterVarsity Press, 2003).

10. Greg Ogden, *Discipleship Essentials*, expanded ed. (Downers Grove, IL: InterVarsity Press, 2007), 10–11.

11. Ogden, *Transforming Discipleship*, 146.

12. David G. Benner, *Sacred Companions* (Downers Grove, IL: InterVarsity Press, 2002).

13. Ibid., 94.

14. Ibid., 166.

15. Ibid., 174.

16. Andy Crouch, *Culture Making* (Downers Grove, IL: InterVarsity Press, 2008), 214.

17. Ibid., 239.

18. Ibid., 246.

CHAPTER 4

19. William D. Mounce, "Love," *Mounce's Complete Expository Dictionary of Old and New Testament Words* (Grand Rapids, MI: Zondervan), 427.

20. Wadell, *Becoming Friends*, 162.

21. He assures those grieving over the death of loved ones not to grieve as those who have no hope, on the basis of the truth that Jesus will come again and all His followers will be reunited.

22. Wadell, *Becoming Friends*, 58.

CHAPTER 5

23. Dietrich Bonhoeffer, *Life Together* (New York, NY: Harper Collins, 1954, 1993), 113.

24. Thomas R. Hawkins, *Cultivating Christian Community* (Nashville, TN: Discipleship Resources, 2004), 36.

25. Ibid., 37.

26. Daniel Taylor, *The Healing Power of Stories* (New York, NY: Doubleday, 1996), 120.

27. Roberta Hestenes, *Using the Bible in Groups*, (Philadelphia, PA: Westminster Press, 1983), 96–97.

28. Larry Crabb, *Soul Talk* (Nashville, TN: Integrity, 2003), 149.

CHAPTER 6

29. Robert Banks, *Paul's Idea of Community* (Peabody, MA: Hendrickson Publishers, 1994), 83.

30. Christine Pohl, *Making Room* (Grand Rapids, MI: Eerdmans, 1999), 74.

31. Gordon T. Smith, *Courage & Calling* (Downers Grove, IL: InterVarsity Press, 2011), 258.

32. Madeleine L'Engle and Luci Shaw, *Friends for the Journey* (Ann Arbor, MI: Servant Publications, 1997), 49.

33. For a more recent treatment of this traditional understanding of the parts of prayer, see Gordon T. Smith, *On the Way* (Colorado Springs, CO: NavPress, 2001), 74–77.

CHAPTER 7

34. Bonhoeffer, *Life Together*, 133–134.
35. Bruce Waltke, *Finding the Will of God* (Gresham, OR: Vision House, 1995), 119.
36. Smith, *Courage & Calling*, 10.
37. Ibid., 68–69.
38. Waltke, *Finding the Will of God*, 128.

CHAPTER 8

39. Paul refers to some key areas of life in his letter to the Ephesians.
   - Church (Ephesians 4:11–16)
   - Family (Ephesians 5:21–6:4)
   - Work (Ephesians 6:5–9)

CHAPTER 9

40. Smith, *On the Way*, 110.
41. Ibid., 130–131.

CHAPTER 10

42. Benner, *Sacred Companions*, 174.
43. Ogden, *Transforming Discipleship*.

EPILOGUE

44. Bronnie Ware, *The Top Five Regrets of the Dying* (Carlsbad, CA: Hay House, 2011, 2012).
45. Ibid., 138.

46. Brother John of Taize, *Friends in Christ* (Mary-
    knoll, NY: Orbis Books, 2012), 124.
47. Ibid., 130.

Since 1985, Soo-Inn has been journeying with people through his ministry of preaching/teaching, writing, and mentoring. Originally trained as a dentist at the University of Singapore, he answered God's call to go into full-time church-related ministry in 1981 and obtained his Master of Theology from Regent College, Vancouver, Canada, in 1984. In 2006, he obtained his Doctor of Ministry from Fuller Theological Seminary, California.

Currently a teaching pastor with Evangel Christian Church, his primary passions include connecting the Word of God to the struggles of daily life and the promotion of the discipline of spiritual friendship. He has been a supporter of Arsenal Football Club since 1971 and his favourite movie is *Star Wars* 4.